THE LAST DAYS OF STEAM IN
THE SCOTTISH
HIGHLANDS

With huge dumb-buffers for shunting around sharp curves, Coatbridge Ironworks 0–4–0ST No. 3 was marshalling wagons at Kipps on 17.8.61. Built by Kitson in the year of Queen Victoria's jubilee, 1887, the diminutive engine exhibited all the fierce energy associated with the Industrial Revolution; the only modern feature to be discerned here was the standard steel 16 ton mineral wagon.

Author

THE LAST DAYS OF STEAM IN
THE SCOTTISH HIGHLANDS

— D. FEREDAY GLENN —

ALAN SUTTON

First published in the United Kingdom in 1991 by
Alan Sutton Publishing Ltd · Phoenix Mill · Stroud · Gloucestershire

First published in the United States of America in 1991 by
Alan Sutton Publishing Inc · Wolfeboro Falls · NH 03896–0848

British Library Cataloguing in Publication Data

Glenn, David Fereday
The last days of steam in the Scottish Highlands.
I. Title
625.261094115

ISBN 0–86299–809–3

Library of Congress Cataloging in Publication Data applied for

Jacket photographs: Front: Built in 1936 by Andrew Barclay, this little 0–4–0ST spent its working life shunting wagons between Cromdale (on the former GNoS Speyside line) and the Balmenach Distillery. This Morayshire scene was pictured in 1961.

colour transparency by J.C. Haydon

Back: Beneath the brooding presence of Ben Nevis, a K1 2–6–0 prepares to cross the Caledonian Canal at Banavie with a train from Fort William to Mallaig.

colour transparency by D. Fereday Glenn

Typeset in 9/10 Palatino.
Typesetting and origination by
Alan Sutton Publishing Limited.
Printed in Great Britain by
The Bath Press, Avon.

Introduction

Between the Solway Firth on the western side and Berwick-upon-Tweed in the east lie the magnificent Cheviot Hills, effectively marking the southern boundary of the ancient Kingdom of Scotland. Few railways pierced the rugged border terrain but beyond, amid the broad sweep of the Lowlands from the Firth of Clyde to the Forth, was the cockpit of

Something of the atmosphere of Glasgow in the 1950s can be glimpsed from this scene in one of the main thoroughfares: three traditional four-wheeled tramcars mingle with the afternoon traffic on 5.9.58, with No. 729 heading westward for Charing Cross and Kelvinside on route 10. On certain parts of the system railway wagons might be conveyed over tram tracks to reach private sidings.

Author

Scottish heavy industry. There were established some of the famous shipyards, with coal mines and steel works nearby to fashion raw materials into the most illustrious liners the world has ever seen. But further north the countryside becomes wilder and more grand, where only a handful of railway lines have managed to endure the harsh environment and changing economic circumstances. Vast tracts of the Highlands have never been served by train, but of those that once were even fewer survive today. To reach Oban, Fort William or Mallaig just a single ribbon of railway runs north from Glasgow, while in the east only two routes continue to Inverness. Yet, despite many difficulties, Dingwall remains the junction for Stromeferry and Kyle of Lochalsh, whereas the Far North line meanders on to Wick and Thurso.

The first diesel multiple units in Scotland began operating between Glasgow and Edinburgh in 1957, with suburban electrification of both North and South Clydeside routes commencing in the 1960s. Main line electrification followed on the West Coast via Shap and Beattock in the early seventies, while the East Coast route will be completed as far as Edinburgh in 1991. Where it is not cost-effective to extend operations 'under the wires', Scot Rail can fall back on the proven ability of Sprinter diesel units to serve the more remote corners of the Highlands for many years to come. But what of steam? Scotland once had a proud heritage of steam locomotive construction – names like Neilson, Dubs, Andrew Barclay and North British spring to mind – but the nationalized railway system abandoned that form of traction before the middle of 1967; only some colliery and private sidings persisted with it beyond then. It was right that the Sassenachs should not have the entire field of steam railway preservation to themselves, so in addition to the Glasgow Museum of Transport three lines have established themselves as havens for artefacts from the past, at Boat of Garten in the Cairngorms, Bo'ness on the Firth of Forth and at Brechin.

But that's not all! Once the vital principle of the revival of main line steam running was conceded by British Rail in October 1971, it was bound to be extended to Scotland in due course. A number of different locomotives and routes have been approved at various times, and it was entirely fitting that steam power should be used to mark the centenary of the Forth Bridge in 1990. But for some years now tourists have been able to ride behind steam over the 'Road to the Isles' (Fort William–Mallaig) on a regular basis, several days each week in the season, with appropriate motive power hauling BR Standard stock – an enlightened policy that must have done wonders for the local economy. For me, the sight of a genuine K1 'Mogul' at the head of 'The Lochaber' as it crossed the Caledonian Canal at Banavie one Sunday in September 1990 was like a time-warp back to my first visit to the Highlands thirty years before – sheer magic!

I am grateful to John Courtney Haydon, who accompanied me on holiday to Scotland in both 1960 and 1961, for the use of certain pictures. Thanks, too, to my son, Miles, for his help with the map and to Margaret Lovell in checking the captions for the photographs, the bulk of which have been selected from my own collection. I hope readers will enjoy them and find much of interest, not least because steam continues to thrive here and there in Scotland.

David Fereday Glenn

THE LAST DAYS OF STEAM IN
THE SCOTTISH
HIGHLANDS

LAST DAYS OF STEAM IN THE SCOTTISH HIGHLANDS
(Only locations relevant to the text are shown)

Locomotive Depots

One of the more interesting changes brought about after the 'Big Four' railway companies were nationalized on 1 January 1948 was a universal system for the recognition of locomotive allocations. The LMS had instigated the idea of a cast metal plate bolted on to the lower part of a steam engine's smokebox door, and this was adopted for the whole of British Railways – though some of the old Company habits persisted in parallel on an unofficial basis until the end of steam. Main locomotive depots were given a code number and letter so that railway employees (and spotters!) could tell at a glance where every individual engine was based, each of the six Regions having a distinctive set of codes. For the Scottish Region these commenced with 60A (for Inverness) and ended with 68E (for Carlisle Canal), including some depots formerly controlled by the LMS and others by the LNER since both had been jointly responsible for the entire passenger network north of the Border. While most depots continued to maintain a distinctive pre-Nationalization 'flavour', this became blurred with the passage of time as aged pre-Grouping designs were withdrawn and modern Standard or diesel engines were drafted in to replace them. A few depots did benefit from a degree of cross-fertilization, but for the majority old loyalties were clearly discernable. Some renumbering of sheds did take place – for example, Fort William began as 65J but became 63B by the 1960s, reflecting a change in the command structure from Eastfield (Glasgow) to Perth; 63B, incidentally, was previously Stirling South. Engines based at a sub-shed normally displayed the code of the main shed on their smokebox doors: if a shed was renumbered or the locomotive reallocated to another depot, it was a simple matter to loosen a couple of bolts to change the cast plate.

My first visit to Scotland occurred during a two-week holiday in what would now be called a minibus, organized by the Gloucestershire Railway Society, in 1958. Never were so many Motive Power Depots visited by a group of fellow enthusiasts in such a short time! There was so much to see one needed to go back again in 1960/1; even then, the sheer magnitude of distance meant it was impossible to go everywhere. Within the limitations of a student's income, primitive transport (a Lambretta scooter in 1960, a 25-year-old Austin Seven in 1961) and by dint of staying overnight at Youth Hostels with the simplest of meals, John Courtney Haydon and I explored Scotland as far north as Dingwall and Strathpeffer. I still have the photographic permit generously provided by Scottish Region, and we were granted access to a number of depots as well. In the Highlands there were few establishments of any size, most being little more than overnight 'dormy sheds' and empty for much of the day (save on Sunday). The really big and important depots were around Glasgow and Edinburgh: who could fail to be impressed with the Gresley streamlined A4 'Pacifics' at Haymarket (64B) or a clutch of 'Princess Coronation' or 'Duchess' 4–6–2s at Polmadie (66A)? But these giants were for the most part associated with the Anglo–Scottish expresses, for a taste of the Highlands one could not do better than board an 18 tram and head for Springburn Road in Glasgow. At Eastfield shed (65A) some of the rugged little engines from the old North British Railway lingered on till very late in the day, while comparable examples from the rival Caledonian Railway could crop up at all manner of places as far afield as Oban or Inverness. Only one example of the Glasgow and South Western Railway survived long enough to be taken into BR stock in 1948, being withdrawn later the same year without being renumbered, and by the latter part of the next decade both the Highland Railway and Great North of Scotland designs were all but eclipsed. And then a miracle happened: four colourful representatives of pre-1923 Scottish railways that had been set aside for the National Collection were put back into working order in all their old finery for occasional steaming on special duties. A pair of ex-Caledonian corridor carriages was also retained, making an appropriate train for the famous Drummond-designed single-wheeler No. 123. These historic locomotives – CR 4–2–2 No. 123, HR 'Jones' Goods' 4–6–0 No. 103, NBR 4–4–0 *Glen Douglas* and GNoS 4–4–0 No. 49 *Gordon Highlander* – came to be based at Dawsholm (65D), a quiet little depot alongside a goods branch near Maryhill (Central) station to the north-west of Glasgow, where the shedmaster could keep a close eye on them. After their brief Indian summer they retired to the Glasgow Museum of Transport, in whose care they have been since the mid-1960s.

And so, before venturing into the more remote parts of Scotland, where all the main passenger services were worked by relatively modern motive power (such as could be found in London any day), some shed visits might not come amiss. At Edinburgh's Dalry Road (64C), for example, North British 0–6–2T and J37 0–6–0 tender engines were to be found lined up beside an array of Caledonian steam power – an ideal introduction to some of the smaller, hard-working types that might otherwise be overlooked. Some of the greatest contrasts, in size, at least, could be discovered during a visit to Grange-mouth (65F) on the Firth of Forth: the depot was home to a number of the gargantuan 8F 2–10–0 locomotives purchased in the post-war period from the MoD for heavy freight traffic. Known, like their more common eight-coupled brethren, as the WD class because of their origins during the Second World War and the fact that most had done a stint abroad as part of the liberation of Europe following the D-Day offensive in 1944, the 2–10–0s were always associated with Scotland after acquisition by BR. Yet the same depot harboured a handful of antique 2F 0–6–0s of the late-Victorian period, looking so quaint with tall stovepipe chimneys and primitive protection against the elements! But perhaps the strangest engines were to be found at sheds like Dunfermline, Kipps, Motherwell, Greenock, St Rollox and St Margarets – little four-coupled saddle-tanks, a number permanently coupled to a prehistoric wooden tender to carry the modest quantities of coal required to keep these 'Pugs' in steam, for there was precious little space to do so on the locomotives themselves. They came from two different sources, these quaint 0–4–0STs, but their purpose (and the tender appendage) was much the same: North British or Caledonian in origin, they mostly ended their days doing light shunting. A favourite task was to be 'Ash Pug', toying with one or two wagons around the ash pits after the bigger engines had had their fires raked through – one particular 'Caley' 0–4–0ST was painted up in full mixed-traffic lining in honour of it being the St Rollox Works shunter.

Perhaps it may be helpful to readers unfamiliar with Scotland in the days of steam, or for the benefit of others who may have hazy memories after all these years, to list the main depots around Glasgow and Edinburgh to which I was introduced on my first visit in 1958.

(a) GLASGOW area	65A Eastfield	66A Polmadie
	65B St Rollox	66B Motherwell
	65C Parkhead	66C Hamilton
	65D Dawsholm	66D Greenock (Ladyburn)
	65E Kipps	
	65F Grangemouth	67A Corkerhill
	65G Yoker	67B Hurlford
(b) EDINBURGH area	64A St Margarets	64D Carstairs (66E)
	64B Haymarket	64E Polmont (65K)
	64C Dalry Road	64F Bathgate
	64G Hawick	

Later codes are shown in brackets, as appropriate.

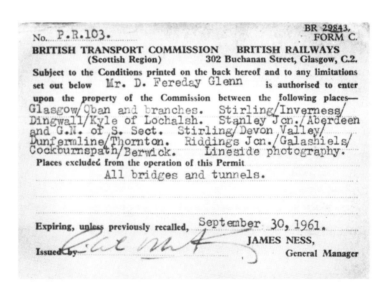

Slightly dog-eared relic from three decades ago, the magic photographic pass for British Railways Scottish Region. Note how, even in 1961, the Speyside line and adjoining routes were still referred to as 'G.N. of S. Sect.' One was allowed to select five routes as a maximum, but branches were included – so Glasgow to Oban encompassed both the Killin and Ballachulish byways as a matter of course!

Author

Designed by Gresley for the Great Northern Railway in 1914, the K2 2–6–0 was a sound mixed-traffic locomotive that adapted well to the demands of the former North British route to Fort William and Mallaig. Most of the regular engines were fitted with side-window cabs to make life easier for the crews, but on 7.9.58 No. 61766 – not one of those so modified – was ex-works on Eastfield shed. In addition to the 40F shed plate (Boston), the depot allocation has been painted on the buffer-beam in traditional LNER style; no doubt the engine was being borrowed by Eastfield for a few duties on the West Highland before heading south to England (and a less arduous existence).

Author

A true West Highland machine, Reid's 6 ft 0 in 4–4–0 was introduced on the NBR in 1913. By 1960 few of the class remained serviceable, but No. 62496 *Glen Loy* of Eastfield was one of the last D34s to be kept in steam for light duties. One of the panels of boiler-cladding did not fit tightly, but the old locomotive had been given an overhead electric warning 'flash' and continued to trundle about like a sewing machine when recorded at its home shed on 4.9.60.

Author

By the late-1930s the West Highland lines needed something more powerful to avoid double-heading, so Gresley produced six three-cylinder 2–6–0s which became LNER class K4. Though excellent over the hilly section when in good condition, their small wheels (only 5 ft 2 in in diameter) were not suited to sustained speed and, by the end of the fifties, the five remaining K4s were moved away to Thornton (62A) and relegated to freight traffic. No. 61994 *The Great Marquess* was in its final season at Eastfield when seen there on 7.9.58.

Author

Numerically the first of Gresley's three-cylinder 2–6–2T engines, introduced from 1930 onwards, No. 67600 was re-boilered and re-classified from class V1 to V3 in the post-war years. Like many of the type, it was based in the Glasgow area for suburban passenger duties but, by 4.9.60 when it was spotted on shed at Eastfield, No. 67600 had been equipped with a control wire and slip-coupling for banking out of Queen Street station up Cowlairs incline. None survive in preservation.

Author

Most locomotive sheds were pretty gloomy inside in steam days – not easy places for an amateur photographer with basic equipment to secure acceptable pictures without flash. The interior of Eastfield was blessed with powerful electric lights so, by resting the camera on a cleaner's trolley, it was possible to obtain a passable time-exposure of class J83 0–6–0T No. 68447. Three of the former North British tanks, introduced by Holmes in 1900, were based at 65A by 4.9.60.

Author

The regular two-cylinder beat of a Stanier 'Black 5' became ever more insistent as it drew steadily nearer and nearer in the gathering gloom: No. 44998 of Perth (63A) was mounting an all-out effort as it passed St Rollox shed with a fitted freight on 17.8.61, the exhaust helping to obscure Glasgow's run-down industrial landscape. In the 'available darkness', the only exposure possible was 1/25th of a second at f6.3; on the adverse gradient the locomotive's speed must have been around 30 mph, so it was a delicate equation when to press the shutter if a photograph was to have any chance of success. . . .

Author

Inside St Rollox depot (65B), only a time-exposure would yield results. Despite a mangled front buffer-beam and twisted frame, 2F 0–6–0T No. 56151 was in steam and ready for another bout of shunting on 17.8.61 – these rugged, outside-cylinder short-wheelbase dock tanks were designed by McIntosh for the Caledonian Railway in 1911 as the 498 class.

Author

Looking very forlorn outside St Rollox shed on 4.9.60 was the last, numerically, of the former CR 'Pugs'. Minus its coal-tender and with cab spectacle glasses smashed, little 0F 0–4–0ST No. 56039 appeared to be an early candidate for scrap. The open-backed cab is illustrated clearly by the ex-SR box van nudging the large dumb buffers behind – no wonder most of the class were equipped with a coal-tender, as there was nowhere to keep it on the engine. Though none survived into preservation, Hornby introduced an attractive '00' scale model to its railway range some years ago to keep their memory alive.

Author

From St Rollox to Parkhead by public transport in the sixties meant a ride by trolley-bus, at least for part of the journey. On arrival the visitor might well be greeted by the sad prospect of a line of steam engines dumped at the end of a siding – as in the sight of K2 2–6–0 No. 61769 on 4.9.60. Though not one of those to have names (all of Highland lochs), No. 61769 was nevertheless of true West Highland lineage as it was fitted with a side-window cab, and Parkhead (65C) was its final depot.

Author

A useful running-in turn for an English-based engine newly overhauled at Cowlairs works was hauling an Engineers' train! Gresley's class J39 0–6–0 No. 64940 was so employed on 4.9.60, while work continued on the Glasgow surburban electrification scheme adjoining Parkhead shed. Some J39s were based north o' the Border, but most of the class were allocated to English depots; Gresley's earlier J38 type, which had smaller driving wheels than the J39, was entirely native to Scotland.

Author

The Caledonian Railway once had a vast fleet of six-coupled goods engines, from the Drummond 'Standard Goods' of 1883 up through the McIntosh '812' around the turn of the century to the final version by Pickersgill after the end of the First World War. Outside Dawsholm shed (65D) on 4.9.60 one of the last type was simmering in the hazy sunlight – 3F 0–6–0 No. 57652 had its tender well stacked with coal and was not long ex-works, as witness the various electric warning flashes on boiler and cab-side.

Author

Inside Dawsholm depot it was rather like Aladdin's cave: four surviving steam engines from the Imperial Age before the Grouping, each in its authentic 'period' livery to add a splash of colour amid all the smudgy black and grey of work-weary locomotives. Perhaps the most striking of them all was the vast bulk of Highland Railway 4–6–0 No. 103 – the 'Jones' Goods' – painted in Stroudley's Improved Engine Green (i.e. a sort of yellow). Built in 1894, this was the first kind of 4–6–0 to run anywhere in Britain. Note the fluted chimney, a feature of many Highland designs.

Author

Dawsholm was one of those Scottish sheds where veterans from a number of different railways, once rivals, could be seen in close proximity. For instance, in this intimate view an old Caledonian 2F 0–6–0 tender engine stands cheek-by-jowl with a former North British 0–6–0T at the mouth of the depot on 4.9.60. The J88 design had driving wheels only 3 ft 9 in in diameter, while its short wheelbase made it ideal for shunting purposes. No. 68336 was in steam and lucky enough to retain the graceful bell-mouthed NBR chimney, while boiler pressure was a mere 130 psi.

Author

Equally typical of Dawsholm's inhabitants was one of the Caledonian 'Pugs'. When the author presented himself to the shed foreman and asked permission to photograph No. 56039 on the end of the store line, he replied in some surprise, 'What, yon wee beetle-crusher?' The 0–4–0ST design was introduced by Drummond in 1885 and continued by McIntosh into the early years of the twentieth century: most had dumb-buffers for shunting round tight-radius curves, and some (like No. 56039) were coupled to ancient wooden coal-tenders.

Author

Also at Dawsholm was stored another HR engine, an inside cylinder 4-4-0 of a type that had penetrated to the extreme far north of Scotland to the twin terminals of Wick and Thurso and the famous Georgemas Junction. Numbered 54398, *Ben Alder* had many features in common with early Drummond designs for the LSWR, but had been designed by Peter rather than Dugald (who migrated south). Sadly, after many years of storage both at Boat of Garten and at Dawsholm, *Ben Alder* was scrapped – had it been sent to Barry for that purpose, the chances are it would have been snapped up, restored and today be running on one of the private lines, but on 17.8.61 no-one knew its fate. . . .

Author

Kipps was the 'Cinderella' of loco sheds in the Glasgow area, for its allocation seemed to consist almost entirely of nineteenth-century relics from the erstwhile North British Railway. Close to Coatbridge (Sunnyside) station, 65E offered the stark contrast between the grimy dregs of a once proud system and the smart new suburban electrics in their distinctive blue livery – remember, this was some years before a different shade of blue became the norm for the whole of BR! On a typically murky day in August 1961 two Holmes 0–6–0s were performing their humble duties beside the overhead masts of the new order: J83 tank No. 68442 shunting wooden-bodied coal wagons in the foreground while an unidentified J36 tender engine waited for its chance to come out of the siding. There was not one diesel in sight!

Author

Class N15 comprised a large number of 0–6–2Ts built for the North British Railway from 1910 onwards for freight and mixed-traffic work. The first six were particularly intended for banking duties up the formidable Cowlairs incline. No. 69126 was the original engine of the series and, no doubt, spent a large part of its life getting to grips with the 1 in 41 out of Glasgow (Queen Street); it was found in more peaceful pose at Dawsholm on 17.8.61.

Author

The rather cramped interior of Dawsholm shed may not have been ideal for photography, but it provided a secure haven for the historic restored locomotives. Youngest of the quartet based there in August 1961 was the GNoS 4–4–0 No. 49 *Gordon Highlander*. Stalwart of the Speyside line, 'The Sojer' remained active on BR until 1958 when it was withdrawn bearing the number 62277 – last survivor of the D40 class and also of the railway company for which it had been constructed by North British in 1920.

Author

The 'Ash Pug' at Kipps. Perhaps the last BR-owned 0–4–0ST in capital stock to be active in Scotland, class Y9 No. 68117 dithers with a couple of 16 ton mineral wagons over the disposal pit on 17.8.61 – note the heap of ash beside the rear wheel. In common with most of the class, No. 68117 is coupled to a vintage wooden 'tender' for its coal supply.

Author

Among the quaint engines at Kipps was a Reid short-wheelbase 0–6–0T with a hideous chimney. In most other respects class J88 No. 68345 was a perfectly normal little shunting loco, albeit with dumb-buffers, but the funnel had a distinctly home-made look about it that did nothing to improve the engine's appearance. Could it have been the inspiration for one of the Revd Awdry's stories?

Author

16

One of the oddities to be discovered at 65E was the 'modernized' J36 0–6–0. The first of what was to become a class of 168 standard goods engines for the NBR appeared in 1888; a number of them distinguished themselves by serving in France during the First World War. Two, both based at Kipps, were modified with cut-down boiler mountings and short chimney for working the Glenbeigh branch – No. 65287 was being coaled up on 5.9.58.

Author

Not far from Falkirk is the oil terminal at Grangemouth, on the Firth of Forth. Grangemouth shed (65F) was the home of some of Scotland's largest locomotives, the ex-WD 8F 2–10–0s numbered between 90750 and 90774. These giants had two counterparts on the Longmoor Military Railway (WD 600/601) in England, while more examples survived further afield. On 4.9.58 No. 90759 was preparing to leave its home shed to take up duty; the near-immaculate condition of this freight locomotive is in sharp contrast to the state of most English-based WD 2–8–0s.

Author

In complete opposition to the 'large loco' image was the sight of a Drummond 'Standard Goods' 0–6–0. More than 200 of these simple, robust machines were taken into Caledonian Railway stock from 1883 onwards; it says much for their good qualities that 140 remained with BR at the end of 1957. Rated 2F by the LMS after 1923, a few were vacuum-fitted for passenger work but No. 57265 of Grangemouth was not one of them; seen going off shed on 4.9.58.

Author

Some idea of the vast bulk of the ten-coupled ex-WD engines can be gained from this broadside angle of 8F No. 90765 in the evening sunlight at Grangemouth on 9.9.60. Note the LNER-style snifting valve behind the short chimney.

Author

The Grangemouth branch from Falkirk was an early candidate for dieselization under the Modernization Plan. Two-car Gloucester RC & W units (with two AEC engines of 150 bhp) of a type introduced in 1957 appeared, but the former Caledonian line had its passenger traffic withdrawn from 29.1.68. In more fortunate times a Grangemouth to Larbert train, consisting of MBS Sc51117 (leading) and composite driving trailer Sc56309, purred past a timber yard opposite 65F shed on 9.9.60; this type of unit was later classified as 100/143.

Author

The recommended method of reaching Yoker (65G) by public transport until 1962 was to catch a No. 9 tram from Argyle Street (in the centre of Glasgow) to Elderslie Bar, then walk along Dyke Road to the shed. On 18.8.61 Corporation tramcar No. 1183 crossed over a narrow bridge – note the 10 mph speed restriction – near Yoker, displaying blinds for Partick and Auchenshuggle. The author's Austin 'Ruby' and the cobbled roadway complete the period picture.

Author

One of the most famous depots in Glasgow was Polmadie (66A), since it served Central station where the express trains to and from Euston, Liverpool, Manchester and other important destinations on the western side of the country departed and arrived. In the 1950s and early sixties it was the shed where exciting named engines were prepared: 'Duchess' 'Pacifics' and 'Royal Scot' 4–6–0s. On 5.9.58 the famed *City of London* 4–6–2 No. 46245 was being prepared for its next journey on the 'Up' 'Royal Scot' express. This handsome locomotive was one of only twenty Stanier 'Pacifics' to be painted in the former LMS red livery for principal express duties; curiously, none of the Scottish-based engines was given this distinctive livery, for they remained in Brunswick green like all other main line passenger motive power.

Author

One of the rather elusive Standard class 6MT 4–6–2s, No. 72004 *Clan Macdonald*, clanks into the loop at Polmadie at the head of a partially-fitted freight from the south on 18.8.61. The 'Clans' were based on the larger and heavier 'Britannia' 'Pacifics', but the difference in weight was negligible and so precluded their use on routes to Fort William, Oban or Inverness; performance was hardly better than the regular class 5 mixed-traffic engines. The first five members of the class were based at 66A and the remainder at Carlisle (Kingmoor). None has been preserved.

Author

Not everything at Polmadie was 'out of the top drawer', for each depot needs shunters as well as 'prima donnas'. On 5.9.58 a former CR 0–6–0T with short wheelbase and outside cylinders was in steam near the huge coaling tower. 2F No. 56154 was a McIntosh design of 1911, doubtless the Caledonian's answer to a North British J88. It is a type that became extinct with steam in Scotland in the sixties.

Author

A much older design that was also wiped out with the abandonment of steam was the CR 'Standard Goods' 0–6–0. No. 57237 is seen at Polmadie shed on 4.9.60. This particular machine was one of the oldest survivors at the time, being built at St Rollox works in 1883. One can only marvel now that veterans like this were part of Scotland's industrial scene for well-nigh eighty years!

Author

In total contrast to the steam age was a controversial diesel-electric locomotive at Polmadie on 4.9.60. Manufactured by Metropolitan Vickers in 1958, D5705 had a Crossley V8 engine that developed 1,200 bhp at 625 rpm. Only twenty of this design were produced for BR, being known as 'Co-Bo' because of the non-matching motor bogies (one having three axles, the other only two). Initially used for the 'Condor' express freight duty between London and Glasgow, the type was soon downgraded to less arduous work due to problems of reliability. The painted shedcode (17A) above the buffer-beam indicates that D5705 was then allocated to Derby. Surprisingly, this machine is today the sole survivor of one of the least successful 'pilot' diesel designs of the Modernization Plan.

Author

Encapsulating the dust and grime always associated with a steam locomotive depot, Standard 4MT 2–6–4Ts Nos 80058 and 80056 'had the road' to back out of the yard towards Eglinton Street and Glasgow Central on 18.8.61. In the background, Polmadie shed (66A) was shrouded in sulphurous fumes while, beyond the signals, gantries for the projected electrification indicated that the sands of time were running out for steam. Truly, the 'last days'.

Author

One would expect some of the 'Royal Scot' class to be based north o' the Border – and at Polmadie, one would not have been disappointed. 7P 4–6–0 No. 46102 *Black Watch* was at 66A on 18.8.61. The appearance of this class was radically altered on rebuilding with Stanier taper boiler, a process begun in 1943 but not completed until more than a decade later. Two examples survive today.

Author

Across the tracks from Polmadie shed, one of the 700-odd ex-WD class 8F 2–8–0s that BR inherited was arriving in a goods reception loop with a train-load of steel tubes, while alongside three 2-car diesel units awaited their next task on 18.8.61. The 2–8–0 was one of those allocated to Polmadie (No. 90640); it had been WD No. 78658 and remained in service until 1966, latterly at Thornton Junction.

Author

South-east of Glasgow lies Motherwell, roughly half-way to Carstairs. Coded 66B, it housed a large number of goods engines for the industrial traffic – but some passenger locos were stored there as well. On 5.9.58 some Pickersgill 3P 4–4–0s were under wraps, looking rather woebegone except for a rough coat of black paint over the smokebox to protect it from corrosion. No. 54465 was one of these: but appearances must have been deceptive, for it was put back into traffic later and used on some enthusiast specials before being scrapped in the early 1960s. Not one of these fine Caledonian 4–4–0s survived.

Author

After the Second World War only two more 4–6–2 locomotives were built for the LMS, both appearing after Nationalization and numbered 46256/7. H.G. Ivatt introduced a few modifications, but to all intents these handsome engines were pure Stanier in design. Last of the line, No. 46257 *City of Salford* was being made ready at Polmadie on 18.8.61.

Author

Among the many goods engines shedded at Motherwell, class 3F (Caledonian Railway '294') 0–6–0 No. 57668 was typical of the breed. This version, in particular, bore more than a passing resemblance to the LBSCR C3 design. Notice the smoke-haze from the locomotives lined up outside the depot!

Author

Blackening an already murky sky, former Caledonian 'Standard Goods' 0–6–0 No. 57326 gives tongue in no uncertain fashion as it passes Motherwell depot with a lengthy train of flat wagons on 16.8.61. These simple and rugged machines were introduced from 1883 by Drummond and continued by both Lambie and McIntosh, with 238 examples entering BR stock in 1948; more than a hundred were still extant in 1961, despite modernization, dieselization or electrification.

Author

The South Clydeside suburban trains were not the first candidates for electrification, so Greenock, Gourock and Wemyss Bay had to wait a while. At Greenock (Ladyburn) shed on 8.9.58 one of the curiosities was a Caledonian 'Pug' – class OF 0–4–0ST No. 56035, complete with obligatory wooden tender for coal. There were two sheds at Greenock, both coded 66D – Ladyburn and Princes Pier – but the latter (sub-shed) closed after withdrawal of the former Glasgow and South Western line's services from Kilmacolm on 2.2.59.

Author

Under clear signals, Standard 4MT 2–6–0 No. 76002 accelerates an assortment of goods wagons past the ash pits at Motherwell depot on 16.8.61. On the right, a WD 8F 2–10–0 locomotive is surrounded by heaps of smoking ash, a reminder of the difficult working conditions experienced by the railwaymen of Scotland's last days of steam.

Author

With its proximity to the Clyde estuary, Greenock had a variety of shunters to deal with local freight traffic and 'trip' working. Former CR '498' class 0–6–0T No. 56173 was just one of the residents at Ladyburn shed, keeping company with a brand-new Barclay 0–4–0D on 3.9.60. The short-wheelbase steam locomotive was withdrawn soon afterwards.

Author

Against the industrial backcloth of the Lower Clyde, a then-new Barclay 0–4–0D No. D2432 trundles along the main line beside Greenock (Ladyburn) shed with a short goods train on 3.9.60. Capable of a maximum speed of 23 mph, this diesel-mechanical shunter had a 5-speed epicyclic gearbox and weighed 37 tons – a far cry from the dirty old steam engines it was due to replace. With the elimination of steam in the late-1960s, this type of shunter became class 06.

Author

Only twenty of the Standard 3MT 2–6–0 design were built, and of these a quarter were shedded at Hurlford (67B). No. 77016 was in light steam at its home base on 18.8.61 – without the help of the smokebox numberplate it would have been difficult to trace the engine's identity, due to the thick layer of grime over the superstructure. Only one member of the class ventured south in its final year (No. 77014 to the Southern Region), the rest spent their entire existence in either Scotland or the North-East.

Author

When former G & SWR locomotives were withdrawn, the vacuum was filled partly with modern LMS designs and partly by ex-CR machines, of which there were ample stocks. Thus on 18.8.61 it came as no surprise to find one of the Pickersgill 3F 0–6–0s (No. 57684) on shed at Hurlford (Kilmarnock). Note the cylinder cover, below the smokebox door, is open to reveal the cylinder heads. This depot and its two sub-sheds (Beith and Muirkirk) were coded 67B in BR days, and this is the plate carried by No. 57684 on the lower part of the smokebox door.

Author

On the former G & SWR section, engines on passenger services continued to display a form of route indicator below the smokebox – illustrated by a southbound departure from Ayr headed by Fairburn 4MT 2–6–4T No. 42131 on 8.9.58. The substantial depot (67C) was alongside the main line. Members of the party and the Bedford 'Workobus' in which they (and the author) travelled from Gloucester can be seen on the left, beside the footbridge to the shed.

Author

A typical train-load of empty coal wagons gets under way past Ayr shed with ex-WD class 8F 2–8–0 No. 90505 in charge on 8.9.58, viewed from the footbridge providing access to the depot. Note the 67C shedplate on the smokebox of No. 90505, while alongside a Fairburn 4MT 2–6–4T (No. 42195) is preparing for a northbound passenger journey to Glasgow (St Enoch). Formerly there was extensive traffic from the Ayrshire coalfield, but many pits have since been closed.

Author

The coaling siding at Ardrossan shed seems to have been affected by a degree of subsidence as ex-CR McIntosh '652' 0–6–0 No. 57627 prepares for its next spell of duty on 3.9.60. A very similar engine (No. 57566) has been preserved and is being restored to working order on the Strathspey Railway at Boat of Garten.

Author

Until modernization and retrenchment eroded their sphere of operations, the south-western corner of Scotland was a stronghold of the Fowler class 2P 4–4–0s. Ardrossan shed (67D) had both Nos 40609 and 40638 on show side by side on 8.9.58. The latter must have been something of a 'pet' since it was still at its home shed two years later and in steam. Note that No. 40638 has managed to retain its original shapely chimney with capuchon, while smokebox numberplate and shedplate have been picked-out in a distinctive style.

Author

Driver's eye view (1): a local service to Kilmarnock makes a sure-footed departure from Ardrossan (Town) station on 3.9.60 behind class 2P 4–4–0 No. 40578, despite the greasy rails after a heavy shower. Behind the tender of McIntosh class 3F 0–6–0 No. 57627 is a short train of tank wagons, plus a couple of barrier or runner vehicles in between the last tank and the brake van.

Author

Driver's eye view (2): past rakes of empty stock a Standard class 3MT 2–6–0 (No. 77015) curves away from Ardrossan (South Beach) with a stopping train to Largs on 3.9.60. Despite some priming, the Standard's exhaust note sounds much sharper than a Fowler or pre-Grouping design, while the small driving wheels – only 5 ft 3 in in diameter – make for quicker acceleration.
It is a pity that not a single example of the 3MT design, tender or tank, has been preserved.

Author

In a steady downpour, the platforms of Ardrossan (South Beach) glisten with water and the station building is reflected in a pool on 3.9.60. Ex-Caledonian class 3F 0–6–0 No. 57627 oozes steam from every pore as it restarts the tank train after a signal check; this particular McIntosh engine is equipped with vacuum brake to work fitted freight or even passenger trains when required.

Author

38

Driver's eye view (3): until the early 1960s Scotland provided the spectacle of a very wide assortment of semaphore signals. This quaint 'scissors' pattern of lower-quadrant signal, possibly of Glasgow and South Western origin, was mounted beneath the canopy of the station at Ardrossan (Town). Both the advertisement and the injunction to cross by the footbridge are worthy of note.

Author

An atmospheric scene inside the shed at Dumfries (68B) shows the sole surviving CR '19' class 0–4–4T No. 55124 at the front. One of the first designs of J.F. McIntosh in 1895, this type had smaller side tanks and coal rails around the top of the bunker. No. 55124 somehow managed to retain its original pattern of chimney, the little engine being sixty years old when pictured on 8.9.58.

Author

At one time both the Caledonian and G & SW railways served the area around Ardrossan but, with the need for economies during the Great Depression, the former CR route was closed in favour of its rival. But although intermediate stations were shut, the terminal at Montgomerie Pier was maintained on a seasonal basis for sailings to and from Belfast or Douglas (Isle of Man). Occasional excursions were run in addition to summer boat trains: on 3.9.60 the famed 'Caley' single-wheeler, 4–2–2 No. 123, headed an authentic train of two restored CR corridor coaches to the pier along the old Caledonian route, seen leaving the closed station of Saltcoates (North). The Montgomerie Pier line was finally abandoned from 6.5.68.

Author

Before the Forth road bridge was constructed a vehicular ferry operated just upstream of the railway bridge; it was from the ferry that this view was obtained on 23.8.61, looking towards South Queensferry. Built in 1890, the Forth Bridge still links Edinburgh with Dundee and Aberdeen, although in the steam age there were branch lines around Dunfermline and Thornton Junction, too. Now illuminated at night, the Forth Bridge celebrated its centenary in some style in 1990 – complete with steam-hauled special train!

Author

At the other end of the scale, it was usual to find at least one example of Holmes' North British 0–4–0ST on shed. Class Y9 No. 68095 was the oldest survivor, and somewhat uncommon in not having a wooden tender permanently attached; when not in use, it was generally parked on one of the short turntable roads at 64A. Luckily, it has been preserved as the sole remnant of its type.

Author

The A2 class consisted of an assortment of engines in several quite distinct batches. The smallest sub-class was the A2/1 comprising just four engines, introduced during the war and incorporating the V2 boiler. No. 60507 *Highland Chieftain* was the first of this group, which followed the six rebuilds of Gresley's 2–8–2s – the P2 class – dating from 1934. Not known as the most successful of the LNER 'Pacific' designs, the position of the outside cylinders is noteworthy. No. 60507 was at St Margarets (64A) on 10.9.60.

Author

On arrival at St Margarets shed in Edinburgh on 4.9.58, class D49 4–4–0 No. 62711 was the first to catch the eye. Named *Dumbartonshire*, it was one of Sir Nigel Gresley's three-cylinder designs with Walschaerts valve gear and massive 6 ft 8 in driving wheels for express passenger work. While the class may have had a reputation for rough riding, it looked every inch a thoroughbred!

Author

Although built for banking work on Cowlairs incline out of Glasgow (Queen Street), class N15 0–6–2T No. 69128 spent a while at Aberdeen (Ferryhill) shed before gravitating to St Margarets. On 24.8.61 it stood alongside the depot in steam, in passably clean condition, while several of the footplate staff enjoyed a break in the sunshine. Note the Westinghouse pump on the smokebox, comparable with push-pull fitted Drummond 'M7' tanks on the Southern.

Author

While some attention from the cleaners would enhance its appearance there is no denying the impressive bulk of a Gresley class V2 2–6–2 at close quarters. No. 60835 was one of only seven of the so-called 'Green Arrows' to be accorded a name: *The Green Howard, Alexandra, Princess of Wales's Own Yorkshire Regiment.* Among their many exploits, the V2s were famed for their work over the Waverley route between Edinburgh and Carlisle via Hawick.

Author

In sparkling form, streamlined class A4 4–6–2 No. 60032 *Gannet* whisks an 'Up' express for London (Kings Cross) through the suburbs of Edinburgh on 10.9.60, watched by one of the local crews from St Margarets depot. Waiting to proceed to Waverley station for a subsequent departure is an English Electric Type 4 diesel locomotive with its 1–Co–Co–1 wheelbase – note the oval buffers in contrast to the well burnished round ones fitted to the A4. *Gannet* carries a 34A shedplate (Kings Cross – Top Shed).

Author

Though a type of loco specially designed by Gresley for Scotland, the class J38 0–6–0 seems to have been rather overlooked. Some of the thirty-five-strong class were rebuilt with the designer's J39-type boiler, like No. 65918 depicted here reversing off St Margarets shed on 16.8.61. With driving wheels only 4ft 8in in diameter, the J38 was a pure freight engine but within its limited sphere of operations it was successful enough to be the last Gresley steam type active north of the Tweed (in 1967).

Author

Of those fortunate enough to have seen Haymarket shed in steam days, who could ever forget that first visit? Despite the appalling lack of light, this little North British tank engine has a special appeal – after some years as one of the Waverley station carriage pilots it was laid aside to await scrap, but the weather revealed evidence of its previous ownership with the tankside exhibiting both 'LNER' and the BR 'hungry lion' emblem. Class J83 0–6–0T No. 68478 was at the back of Haymarket depot on 3.9.58 and was scrapped soon after.

Author

Another J83 that remained active at Edinburgh until the sixties was No. 68481. Despite a layer of grime, its former status as carriage pilot was evident from both the vacuum brake fitting and full lining out on tanksides and bunker when located in steam at 64B on 10.9.60. The loss of one front buffer did not seem to impair its usefulness in dealing with wagons of loco coal! This kind of engine was immortalized some time ago when Triang-Hornby had a 4mm scale model of the J83 – painted in LNER apple green – in their range.

Author

Classified as 'OF' by BR, the ex-NBR class J88 0–6–0T was small indeed. With dumb-buffers and a short wheelbase it was to be expected that such an engine would spend its life shunting – the amazing thing was how many years the class continued to perform that function. The oldest survivor at Haymarket shed on 10.9.60 was No. 68320, which retained the Reid pattern of tall, shapely chimney to the end; it was built in 1904.

Author

Another survivor from a bygone age was still very active on 3.9.58. Classic North British 4–4–0 No. 62467 *Glenfinnan* had just been serviced at Haymarket and was about to make for Waverley station, before returning to Thornton depot (62A) with a local passenger train. After the fashion of a number of named Scottish steam engines, the name was painted on the driving-wheel splasher.

Author

In spite of extensive dieselization, the summer timetable provided some opportunities for steam power to show what it could do. On 16.8.61 class A3 4–6–2 No. 60073 *St Gatien* smartly accelerated a westbound train from Edinburgh Haymarket station past the loco depot (64B) with an assorted rake of passenger stock. This Gresley Pacific had recently received a double chimney and Witte (German) style smoke deflectors, but kept its GNR type of tender – it made an interesting comparison with the English Electric Type 4 (class 40) diesel-electric machine on the left of the picture.

Author

No album on Scottish steam would be complete without a picture of – arguably – one of the most celebrated survivors from the nineteenth century. Class J36 0–6–0 No. 65243 was just one among a class of more than 100 elderly goods engines that entered the ranks of BR in 1948, but not only was it one of that select group to have been named in connection with the First World War but it was allocated to Haymarket shed in 1920 and stayed there till it closed! Better known these days as *Maude* (named after a distinguished officer who served with the Coldstream Guards), No. 65243 had just come on shed at 64B on 3.9.58 to be prepared for the next day's work when it was snapped *without* its name. Built by Neilson in 1891, this fine old engine is now preserved at Bo'ness on the Firth of Forth, only a few miles from its old haunts.

Author

Sandwiched between an aged NBR 0–6–0 and a double-chimney class A3 4–6–2 (No. 60098 *Spion Kop*), Thompson B1 4–6–0 No. 61246 represents a useful mixed-traffic design that had the distinction of operating on every Region of BR between 1942 and 1967. Several named B1 locos were based in Edinburgh, either at St Margarets or Haymarket: No. 61246 commemorated *Lord Balfour of Burleigh*, being pictured at 64B on 10.9.60.

Author

Another survivor from the last days of Scottish steam is *Blue Peter*. Built just after Nationalization in 1948 as one of the final – and most successful – of the mixed-traffic class A2 'Pacifics', No. 60532 became a household word when its name was adopted by a children's television programme in the sixties. At the time of writing it is undergoing a thorough refit to enable it to re-enter traffic in the nineties, in the authentic Brunswick green livery it carried throughout its working life; it is the sole example of a Peppercorn 4–6–2 to exist today.

Author

'Top Shed' north o' the Border! A typical line-up at Haymarket on 16.8.61 comprised: Gresley class A4 'Pacific' No. 60024 *Kingfisher*; 'Green Arrow' mixed traffic class V2 2–6–2 No. 60865; a B1 4–6–0, with tender only visible, plus an unidentified English-Electric Type 4 diesel. *Kingfisher* was one of the last A4s to remain at work, ending its days on the Aberdeen–Glasgow three-hour trains before heading south to power a handful of excursions on unfamiliar territory in 1966.

Author

Like Glasgow, Edinburgh once boasted an extensive tramway system. The main conversion programme got under way during the early 1950s, with total abandonment by the end of 1956. This late view shows a flat-roofed example (car No. 94) negotiating a curve beneath the railway on route 13; the destination reads 'Church Hill'.

Lens of Sutton

Dalry Road depot in Edinburgh housed a motley collection of steam engines. One of the small class of 2F 0–6–0T locos introduced by the LMS in 1928, No. 47163, was based there – it looked something like a 'Jinty' with cut-away side tanks and outside cylinders, plus a short wheelbase. In many respects it was a modernized version of the Caledonian '498' shunting tank designed by McIntosh but with driving wheels one inch smaller. No. 47163 was in steam on 3.9.58, surrounded by true Scottish machines.

Author

Dalry Road (64C) was home to a former North British class J37 0–6–0 No. 64612, as well as sundry ex-Caledonian relics, on 3.9.58. The J37 was one of the most powerful pre-Grouping designs, being 5F in BR days; its simple, straightforward concept served the North British, LNER and British Railways well for half a century, particularly on freight from the Fife coalfields.

Author

This contrast in ex-Caledonian front-ends was to be seen at Dalry Road on 3.9.58. In full view just outside the shed was McIntosh 0–6–0 No. 57565, while the higher-boilered Pickersgill design was represented by No. 57654; both were classified 3F by the LMS (and BR). Note the smoky atmosphere around the depot, reminiscent of Motherwell or Kipps!

Author

On a fine summer day another McIntosh class 3F 0–6–0 (No. 57634) was parked out of steam at the end of a siding. Although most of the engine's external appearance could only be described as shabby, the smokebox and chimney as well as the shedplate (64C) had received recent attention to keep it fit for work. Note the matchboard-sided vehicle alongside, perhaps part of the breakdown train.

Author

An older version of the Caledonian class 3P 4-4-0 is represented by No. 54461, on shed at Carstairs (64D) on 5.9.58. In steam and quite clean, the tender-full of coal indicates there must have been regular employment for such an engine in the late-fifties, probably on local services to either Glasgow or Edinburgh.

Author

At Carstairs station one of the LMS-built class 2P 0-4-4Ts, No. 55261, was on station pilot-duty on 5.9.58. The clean condition and traditional CR-style chimney (rather than the more familiar stovepipe) make this a particularly attractive little locomotive. Note the class 'A' headcode! Though Carstairs shed was 64D at this date, it was later renumbered 66E.

Author

Polmont is another shed that changed its identity during the BR era. Close to a canal tow-path, the depot was initially coded 64E, but was denoted 65K in the sixties. On 4.9.58 class B1 4–6–0 No. 61277 came under the bridge west of Polmont station with a semi-fast train for Falkirk (Grahamston), a duty that had not then been dieselized.

Author

Bathgate remained on the railway map of Scotland largely due to the motor manufacturing plant nearby. As long ago as 1961, the British Locomotive Shed Directory advised readers that 'the shed is on the north side of the line east of Bathgate (Upper) station – closed'. On 4.9.58 a rather forlorn class J36 (right) and J35 0–6–0 No. 64484 were in residence at 64F; the J35 was a less-powerful version of the J37, having smaller cylinders. This particular engine had slide valves, whereas some J35s and all the J37s had piston valves.

Author

By the summer of 1961 it was difficult to find any pre-Grouping 4-4-0s at work in Scotland – most were in store out of use or awaiting scrap. Inside the small shed at Hawick (on the wonderful Waverley route) one of the vanishing 'Glen' D34s was kept in reserve, just in case. As it was impossible to photograph inside, a kindly railwayman arranged for the shunter to propel it out through the end door! In the gathering dusk No. 62484 *Glen Lyon*, almost the last of its kind, was recorded on 15.8.61 at 64G: 'Nae more to ride the Road to the Isles, just one last trip to the breakers' yard.'

Author

The last 4–4–2 tender locomotive in BR stock ran in 1958. The tank versions lasted only a year or two longer before succumbing to their fate: in Scotland the final examples were those designed by Reid for the North British Railway (LNER classes C15/C16). At Longniddry, a sub-shed of Edinburgh St Margarets (64A), class C16 4–4–2T No. 67497 looked forlorn on 3.9.58, stored in the company of some D11 'Scottish Director' 4–4–0s.

Author

Part of the furniture at Dunfermline shed was the erstwhile NBR 0–4–0ST No. 68101, complete with wooden tender. By 9.9.60 it was past redemption, with coupling rods removed and dumped at the end of a siding outside the shed. Coded 62C, Dunfermline was not far from Edinburgh but on the north side of the Firth of Forth.

Author

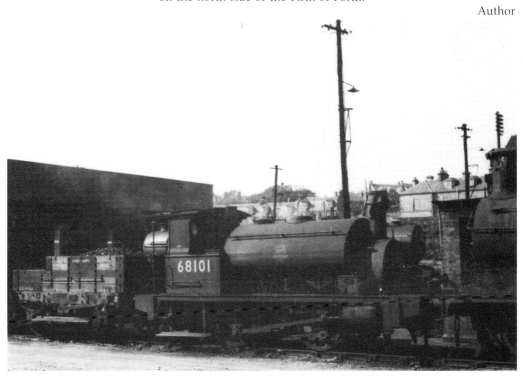

Even in 1958, the North British 'Pug' at Dunfermline (class Y9 0–4–0ST No. 68101) spent most of the time in store. This shed scene on 4.9.58 shows the stovepipe chimney covered over but with engine and aged wooden coal tender otherwise intact. In the background an 8F 2–8–0 (ex-WD) simmers in the sunshine, contrasting with the blackness of the interior of the flat-roofed shed.

Author

Well-positioned to serve the needs of the Fife coalfield, Thornton junction (62A) had a fascinating allocation. While freight predominated, there were some local passenger duties to the east of the Ochil hills until line closures and dieselization took their toll. One of the engines affected by these changes was 'Scott' class D30 4–4–0 No. 62442 *Simon Glover*. A former NB design with 6 ft 6 in driving wheels, the type became extinct in 1960.

Author

Another class of 4–4–0 to be decimated during the fifties was the D11/2. Introduced in 1924 as a post-Grouping development of a proven Great Central design, with lower boiler mountings to suit restricted clearances north of the Tweed, the 'Scottish Directors' were handsome and capable engines for passenger work. On 4.9.58 No. 62678 *Luckie Mucklebackit* must have been one of the last to be in steam, idly shunting a wagonload of ash at Thornton – not the most suitable task for a high-stepping performer with 6 ft 9 in driving wheels! Note the private-owner coal wagon, formerly belonging to Read & Son.

Author

A number of the rugged J38 class of 0–6–0 tender engines were based at Thornton. No. 65931 was one that retained its original pattern boiler, found standing coupled to another member of the class outside the shed on 9.9.60. This Gresley design lingered to the very end of steam in Scotland, still pulling the coal trains for which it was intended when introduced in 1926.

Author

When the Gresley three-cylinder class K4 2–6–0s were withdrawn from the West Highland line in 1958, they went to Thornton for freight work. The neat lines of the first of the class, No. 61993 *Loch Long*, can be appreciated from this view at Thornton on 9.9.60, though it would appear the engine was under repair at the time. Only No. 61994 *The Great Marquess* survives, now restored to full working order with its original LNER number 3442.

Author

Thornton could be relied upon for almost every kind of North British freight engine, including the class J35/5 variant. No. 64472 was one of this smaller sub-class, which had been designed with piston valves from the beginning, like its bigger and more powerful cousin the J37. This version had been designed by Reid in 1906, having 18¼ in diameter cylinders as opposed to the 19½ in of the J37; in BR days the difference in power between the two was marked by the J35 being 3F compared to the 5F classification adopted for the J37 0–6–0. In the background an ubiquitous class B1 4–6–0 (No. 61148) waits its next call to duty on 9.9.60.

Author

From 1957 a North British design of 0–4–0D shunter was introduced in quite large numbers. Classified as DY11 by former LNER sheds, the series of seventy-two engines began with No. 11708 but, before the order was completed, renumbering from D2708 onwards came into force. At Dundee (Tay Bridge) depot a batch of these powerful little machines took over much local shunting work from steam – No. 11712 was typical on 4.9.58, with original style BR emblem on the bonnet sides. In due course it was renumbered D2712; Tay Bridge was 62B.

Author

A sign of the times at Thornton on 4.9.58 was the arrival of brand-new 0–6–0D D2577. Built by Hunslet, it was one of a number of diesel-mechanical shunters employing the tried and tested Gardner 8L3 type engine, which developed 204 bhp at 1,200 rpm, coupled to a four-speed gearbox. Later designated '05', this type was known by the former LNER depots and workshops as class DJ13. Note the hardly-scuffed oval buffers, with '204' chalked on the left-hand one, and the vacuum brake pipe. In the background, the 62A coaling-stage dominates the skyline – a poignant contrast of old and new.

Author

In open country near Markinch a grubby class J37 wheeled a long string of empty mineral wagons from Dundee to Thornton junction on a hot summer afternoon. Apart from a wisp of steam from the safety valves in front of the cab No. 64557 might appear inert, but the sturdy engine was actually travelling at around 30–35 mph as it passed the members of the permanent way gang at work on the other track. An ex-SR 25T brake van, far from home, was coupled next to the tender on 9.9.60.

Author

Kittybrewster shed (61A) at Aberdeen was the place to go to see an elusive quartet of former Great North of Scotland engines, used for shunting the docks at the 'Granite City'. Class Z4 0–4–2T No. 68191 was one of two with 3 ft 6 in driving wheels that lasted until 1959, the other pair (Z5) had larger driving wheels, but all four were built by Manning-Wardle in 1915.

R.H.G. Simpson

With a headcode disc reminiscent of the GE Section or Southern practice, ex-GNoS class Z5 0–4–2T No. 68192 basks in the sunshine at Aberdeen (Kittybrewster shed) among some elderly NB 0–6–0s. This Manning-Wardle design had 4 ft 0 in driving wheels and weighed just under 31 tons. It was scrapped in 1960.

R.H.G. Simpson

Gateway to the West Highlands

Buchanan Street station was the terminus for trains to Stirling, Perth, Forfar and Aberdeen; there were also services to the West Coast via the Callander and Oban route. This was the former Caledonian Railway terminus, so it was entirely appropriate that an excursion graced by the restored CR 'Single' No. 123 should commence from here. The immaculate old engine, with burnished copper and brasswork setting off its fine blue livery, made a stately exit from Buchanan Street with matching rolling stock on 6.9.58, the tender piled high with choice lumps of coal. The station closed in November 1966.

Author

All the main railway termini in Glasgow were situated within one square mile of the city centre. A passenger arriving at Central station from, say, London (Euston) would have been greeted with sights like this – at least until late 1961 – on emerging into Hope Street. On the left a No. 29 tram (bogie car 1215) passes the building society on the corner of Bothwell Street while a No. 54 motor bus (Corporation Leyland 'Titan' L42; FYS 665) bound for Crookston clatters over the cobbles as it tries to overtake on the inside. Glasgow Corporation trams ceased in 1962.

Author

Queen Street station, with its fearsome ascent of Cowlairs incline, remains the main terminal for West Highland line trains. Apart from the changed motive power and blue and grey carriage livery services continued much as before into the 1980s. Ardlui (for Loch Lomond) still retained semaphore signals when 'Up' and 'Down' West Highland trains passed there in September 1974, while most rolling stock continued to be Standard Mark I corridors – introduced in steam days back in the fifties, and still steam-heated! BRCW diesel-electric locomotive 27.043 (originally D5414 when new in 1961/2) headed the Glasgow–Fort William train on the right, while 27.037 (D5389) waited for the single line southward to Glasgow.

Author

Almost 60 miles from Glasgow (Queen Street), the 1005 to Fort William and Mallaig storms out of Crianlarich (Upper) on 5.9.60 refreshed and ready for the 6-mile climb to Tyndrum summit. Double-headed by a matched pair of 5MT engines with Standard 4–6–0 No. 73109 leading Stanier No. 44996, the heavy train includes both restaurant coach and observation car. The single track to the right used to be the goods loop between Crianlarich (Upper) and (Lower) stations, but since closure of the former CR route between Dunblane and the latter point it has been upgraded for all Oban traffic.

Author

The observation car at the rear of the 1005 from Glasgow (Queen Street) to Fort William disappears out of sight after leaving Crianlarich (Upper) on 5.9.60. This carriage was one of a pair converted from pre-war LNER 'Beaver-tail' cars used in the special 'Coronation' trains – note the BR emblem on the fascia below the observation windows.

Author

Blasting up the short 1 in 66 gradient southbound from Crianlarich (Upper), Stanier 'Black 5' 4–6–0 No. 44975 had charge of the Fort William to Glasgow freight on 5.9.60. Once over the top, the crew could look forward to an easy run mostly downhill as far as Arrochar and Tarbet. Although originally a LMS design, these Stanier engines became strongly associated with the West Highland line during the last years of steam, both on passenger and freight traffic.

Author

The SYHA hostel at Crianlarich was a useful place to stay to see the early morning and overnight trains from the south. On a murky Saturday morning the 0510 from Glasgow (Queen Street) to Fort William slithered away from Crianlarich (Upper) as both 5MT 4–6–0s spun their wheels on the wet rails. At about half-past seven and with an autumnal mist reducing the light, this picture of Nos 73105 and 44929 had to be taken at 1/75th of a second on 400 ASA film.

Author

On Saturday mornings the sleeping cars from London (Kings Cross) to Fort William ran as a separate train direct from Edinburgh, leaving at 4.30 a.m.; arrival at Crianlarich was supposed to be 7.51 a.m. On 19.8.61 only a single Standard 5MT 4–6–0 was available and, by the time it had taken water, No. 73109 left the Upper station rather late. With some slipping on the damp rails, the Standard 5 made a rousing departure from the island platform but having the prospect of a difficult journey across Rannoch Moor ahead.

Author

Between Crianlarich and Tyndrum the former Caledonian and North British lines run parallel, roughly one mile apart. Then the NB route turns north towards Bridge of Orchy, sweeping round in a great horseshoe curve. A Fort William–Glasgow (Queen Street) train, probably headed by a Stanier 'Black 5', is dwarfed by the sheer mass of Beinn Dorain (3,523 ft) as it heads south on 19.8.61.

Author

Something of the vast wildness of the Grampian Mountains can be glimpsed from the carriage window at Corrour station, not far from Loch Ossian. A freight train with BRCW 27.004 in charge waits in the loop while an afternoon passenger service from Fort William to Glasgow runs into the other platform on 4.9.74. Island platforms like this are particularly common on the West Highland.

Author

With the North British lower-quadrant signal clear, Stanier 'Black 5' 4–6–0 No. 44975 is opened up to some purpose at the approach to Crianlarich (Upper) station with a goods from Fort William on 5.9.60. On the left is the connecting link to the Callander and Oban section of the former Caledonian Railway – which ran at a lower level more or less at right-angles to the NB route. Crianlarich (Lower) station closed prematurely on 28.9.65 because of a landslip on the section between Crianlarich and Dunblane, although it was already under threat of abandonment from 1.11.65 anyway; thereafter, the trains for Oban used the Upper station and thence over the spur to regain the CR line.

Author

Spean Bridge did not have an island platform like most other stations on the West Highland line. Once it was a junction: the Highland and North British shared a branch line through Gairlochy and Invergarry to Fort Augustus, but it lost money and closed on 1.12.33. Today Spean Bridge retains much of its original charm and remains open as a passing place between Tulloch and Fort William.

Lens of Sutton

Preparations for a new station were already begun when this picture was taken in 1974: BRCW diesel-electric 27.040 had uncoupled and moved clear of the stock of a Glasgow–Fort William train while another of the same type hooked on ready to return south. The original Fort William terminus was replaced in 1975 and trains are now berthed closer to the junction.

Author

The oldest steam locomotive by 1960 to be based at Fort William shed (coded 65J at first, later 63B) was No. 65313. Designed for the Victorian Age, this simple J36 0–6–0 tender engine acted as station pilot, a very necessary function for a terminal when all trains were loco-hauled. Against the backcloth of the hills beyond Loch Linnhe, old No. 65313 was off to get another rake of carriages shunted back into the station on 7.9.60.

Author

Although the railway track continued beyond the station at Fort William along the quayside, this area and the adjoining pier were largely the preserve of David MacBrayne's buses. This view, taken immediately outside the station forecourt, shows some of the local MacBrayne's fleet during the 1950s – AEC, Maudslay and Bedford buses were typical – which also were licensed to carry the mails. Choppy waters in Loch Linnhe and a damp forecourt are still commonplace.

R.H.G. Simpson

Built in 1937 as the last but one of the Gresley three-cylinder class K4 2–6–0s, *MacCailin Mor* was rebuilt by Thompson in 1945 as a two-cylinder machine. As such it became the prototype for Peppercorn's new and slightly longer K1 series numbered 62001 upwards, several of which were regular performers on the West Highland Extension. Numbered 61997, the solitary K1/1 stayed on the Fort William–Mallaig line after its three-cylinder brethren were transferred to Thornton for a more humdrum existence hauling freight, being withdrawn during the summer of 1961. In its last year, *MacCailin Mor* had steam at full pressure as it began to move off shed at Fort William on 7.9.60.

Author

Observation cars were a feature of both sections of the West Highland line, and these required turning on the turntable just like the steam locomotives. On the evening of 19.8.61 class J36 0–6–0 No. 65313 was retrieving car E1719E from the turntable at Fort William after it had been turned in preparation for the next day's 0955 working to Mallaig. Next to the shed building, class K1 2–6–0 No. 62031 had a good head of steam that belied its shabby exterior – Highland extremes of weather did not encourage much more than essential maintenance!

Author

With rain clouds gathering over the Ben, the aged J36 0–6–0 No. 65313 carefully shunted one of the two 'Beaver-tail' observation cars (E1719E) towards Fort William station after it had been turned on the shed's turntable. A former LNER fish van – piped for use with passenger trains – stood in the yard, possibly in transit from Mallaig to one of the big cities in England. The date was 19.8.61.

Author

The Mallaig–Fort William goods was entrusted to class B1 4–6–0 No. 61134 on 7.9.60. The fact that it consisted of just four wagons and a brake van did not augur well for the future of freight on the West Highland Extension. The LNER-designed B1 was the equivalent of Stanier's 'Black 5' on the LMS, but both types were equally at home around Fort William, where this picture was taken.

Author

Mallaig in the nineties: 'Glens' and 'Lochs' have long gone, like the fish traffic, but a fairly basic service still runs seven days a week. Typical of today's train is the class 156 Super Sprinter diesel, but from May till September tourists are tempted by the ageless appeal of steam – two engines spend the season based at Fort William to work 'The Lochaber'. In the absence of any turntables, the locos operate chimney-first to Mallaig and tender-first on the way back; semaphore signals have vanished along the West Highland Extension since radio signalling came into force at Banavie (even the steam engines are fitted with aerials!). Unit 156.449 waits at Mallaig on 3.9.90 to form the 1030 departure to Glasgow (Queen Street); the 'steamer' is due in at 1215 behind K1 2–6–0 No. 2005 (62005) of Fort William shed. Can this *really* be 1990?

Author

The Callander and Oban line finally opened throughout in 1880, but an important part of it – from the southerly junction at Dunblane to the connecting link at Crianlarich (Lower) – was closed by a landslip near Glenoglehead on 28.9.65. This was prophetic, since closure notices had been posted for 1 November that year anyway! In happier times an unadvertised school train ran from Callander as far as Luib: it was nothing fancy, just a single carriage was sufficient. On 5.9.60 LMS-built class 2P 0-4-4T No. 55263 was in charge as it galloped down the 1 in 70 from Glenoglehead towards Killin Junction, the Caledonian style of engine leaving a trail of acrid smoke in its wake.

Author

Through Glen Dochart, right beside the main A85 road was the tiny station of Luib. This, too, was affected by the premature abandonment of all services due to the landslip on Glenoglehead in September 1965. But on 5.9.60 Luib and the erstwhile CR route to Oban played host to the goods from Glasgow: 'Black 5' 4–6–0 No. 45159 of St Rollox shed (65B) had just set back to pick up the scholars' carriage from the loop before accelerating away for the West Coast with characteristic bark. The appearance of a 'mixed' train ceased on arrival at Crianlarich (Lower), where the coach was detached and remained until next morning.

Author

Today, trains from Glasgow (Queen Street) divide at Crianlarich for Fort William and Mallaig or Oban, the latter using the curve from the NB station to join the former Callander and Oban route just to the west of what used to be Crianlarich (Lower). On 5.9.60 class 5MT 4–6–0 No. 44972 followed the spur with a goods for Oban five years before it became the route for passenger traffic on closure of the Callander line, gently descending from Crianlarich (Upper) with Stob Garbh and Ben More in the background.

Author

Double sentinels warned of the approach to Crianlarich from the west in 1960: on the left of the single ribbon of track from Oban stood a modern upper-quadrant distant signal of a pattern familiar over much of the London Midland Region of British Railways at that time. The 'X' straddling the arm was to indicate to drivers that they should ignore the signal as it was not yet in use. The taller, lower-quadrant signal to the right was typical of the Caledonian tradition with wooden arm and massive metal spectacle-plate – notice also the lattice post in contrast to the modern tubular design beside it. The picture was taken on 5.9.60, with the new signal replacing the old just a few weeks later. It is pleasing to be able to record that the CR signal arm was purchased from BR by John Courtney Haydon and is now preserved.

Author

Byway to Loch Tay

The tourists' view of Killin: for those who ventured off the beaten track and had the time to linger at such outposts of British Railways' empire, the result was worth the effort. There were economies, of course, with a single line, a single carriage, one engine in steam and no run-round loop! While No. 55173 waited in the small goods yard, the guard allowed the coach to gently gather speed thanks to gravity in the direction of Loch Tay. After applying the hand-brake, the 'Caley' tank would emerge from the yard and couple on the other end – simple when you know how. Meall nan Tarmachan provided the backdrop at no extra cost.

Author

By the sixties there were only two branch lines left off the main route between Callander and Oban. The first of these was from Killin junction to the shores of Loch Tay: the junction was an 'exchange platform' only, as it had no road access, while the little terminus by the loch side had closed at the outbreak of war in September 1939. In such constrained circumstances the surviving 4¼ miles from the junction to Killin boasted just five trains each way on Mondays to Saturdays; there was no service on Sundays. The sixty-year-old McIntosh '439' class 0–4–4T No. 55173 was bound for Killin with the 10.28 service from Killin junction where the branch crossed over the A85 on 19.8.61.

Author

Former Caledonian Railway '439' 0–4–4T No. 55173 arrives at Killin station on 19.8.61 with the 'mixed' from Killin junction – the usual non-corridor carriage plus one van. A handful of passengers engage the attention of the staff, probably a general factotum who both issued and collected tickets, acted as porter, station-master and shunter all rolled into one. Here, surely, was the archetypal branch terminus against the backcloth of Glen Ogle and the Breadalbane hills!

Author

With tanks and bunker full, 2P 0–4–4T No. 55173 shuffled along through the woods to pick up its train again. Built for the Caledonian Railway in 1901 with surprisingly large 5 ft 9 in driving wheels, the '439' class had been so successful on passenger trains that the design was continued by the LMS after the Grouping. This idyllic scene beside Loch Tay was recorded on 19.8.61: within a year the 'Caley' tanks were gone, being replaced by Standard 4MT 2–6–4Ts of the 800xx series. After 28.9.65 the branch was no more. . . .

Author

Though Loch Tay station had become a private residence following withdrawal of the passenger service beyond Killin, the track remained in situ. In fact, it was used daily since the tiny locomotive depot was located right at the very end of the line. There was no water column at Killin, so the branch engine made the 1 mile pilgrimage to the loch whenever replenishment was needed. On 19.8.61 two 16T wagons supplied the loco with coal after its tanks were filled.

Author

The deliciously decadent character of the Killin branch is summed-up more truthfully, perhaps, in this one picture than in any number of words. On 5.9.60 class 2P 0–4–4T No. 55263 was plodding wearily up from Killin towards the junction with the afternoon train, the sulphurous pall of smoke visible for miles. The post-Grouping version of the Caledonian's '439' tank was not in the prime of life, the ganger had been economical with track maintenance on this section of the line and an autumnal chill was blowing down the Glen. . . .

Author

Branch Line to Ballachulish

Though, even in 1961, Scottish Region was promoting Fort William as the station for Ballachulish, Glencoe and Kinlochleven (MacBrayne's buses), anyone bothering to take the trouble could discover that it was possible to reach Ballachulish by train. Direct it might not have been, but possible – yes! From Oban the branch train followed the main route as far as Connel Ferry, then curved away northward to cross the narrow neck of Loch Etive at the point known as Falls of Lora. Here was built one of the minor wonders of the world – the cantilever Connel Ferry Bridge. On 6.9.60 former CR 0–4–4T No. 55224 crossed the single line over the bridge amid squally showers, bound for Ballachulish.

Author

Not even listed in the main body of the published timetable, Barcaldine Halt only warranted a footnote. Nevertheless, it was served by all the branch trains despite its lowly status. The crew of the 12.26 from Ballachulish peered out in some surprise when a group of Sassenachs invaded the place, leaving their scooters on the tiny platform in order to take photographs! The engine was former CR 'Standard Goods' 0–6–0 No. 57345, specially fitted with vacuum brake in order to work passenger trains in this remote corner of Argyllshire.

Author

With the old engine hissing steam in all directions, 2F 0–6–0 No. 57345 eased its three-coach, 100 ton train away from Barcaldine Halt with the 12.26 Ballachulish to Oban service on 6.9.60. A couple of wagons occupied the siding, perhaps to await the following goods train – unlike Killin, the 27-mile-long Ballachulish branch was not worked on the 'one engine in steam' principle.

Author

After drifting through the curve at Creagan, McIntosh 0–6–0 No. 57571 responded to the regulator as it headed south with the pick-up goods from Ballachulish on 6.9.60. The overgrown sidings and washed out ballast indicated some backlog of maintenance, but the former CR branch closed to all traffic on 28.3.66.

Author

Close to the shoreline of Loch Linnhe, the branch goods from Ballachulish to Oban beats up against the prevailing wind coming in from the Atlantic on a cold September day in 1960. Class 3F 0–6–0 No. 57571 was designed by McIntosh for the Caledonian Railway around the turn of the century, this particular example being equipped with vacuum brake for working passenger or fitted freight.

Author

While much of the line ran alongside Loch Linnhe, the terminal at Ballachulish was actually beside Loch Leven. Beyond the neat, single-storey station building that straddled both platforms was the mass of Meall Mor and the quarry. A former CR '439' class 0–4–4T, No. 55224, waited hopefully for some passengers for the 3.57 p.m. departure for Oban on 6.9.60 for there was always the chance of a busload from Kinlochleven, at the head of the loch, while others might cross on the ferry and join the train at the next station.

Author

As the storm clouds gather over Glencoe, class 2P 0–4–4T No. 55224 follows the waters' edge beside the A828 road as it heads south with the 3.57 p.m. from Ballachulish to Oban on 6.9.60. The south-westerly wind whisks the exhaust away from the stovepipe chimney towards the mountains while, in the background, small settlements huddle together in defiance of the inhospitable climate: this was the six-days-per-week reality of the last days of steam on the West Coast of Scotland.

Author

Stirling, Perth and the Forfar Route

A brace of Perth (63A) engines – Standard 5MT 4–6–0s Nos 73009/73006 – approach Stirling past the locomotive depot with an express on 5.9.58. Although it is not known where the train was bound, the fact that it was double-headed for a load not much exceeding 300 tons might indicate the Highland main line to Inverness. On that route crews were faced with the formidable ascents of Drumochter and Slochd, the former being nearly 1,500 ft above sea level.

Author

By then the oldest survivor of the McIntosh inside-cylinder 0–6–0Ts, class 3F No. 56232 was based at Stirling shed (65B). On 5.9.58 it had class 'A' headlamps in position, but this may have been just a touch of local humour for it was engaged in shunting cattle vans alongside Stirling station. Note the odd position of the shedplate, above the front numberplate.

Author

One of the Polmadie 'Clans', class 6MT 4–6–2 No. 72003 *Clan Fraser*, was in charge of the Perth to London (Euston) service at Stirling on 5.9.58. Leaving Perth at 9 a.m., the train did not reach London until 7.40 p.m., so it was just as well it conveyed both buffet and restaurant cars for long-distance passengers.

Author

Perth shed (63A) had several engines in store, like this CR Pickersgill '72' class 4–4–0 on 5.9.58. Despite the seeming hopelessness, this particular engine, No. 54485, was one of a pair of these handsome locomotives to be specially prepared for film sequences on the old Highland main line between Perth and Aviemore in 1960 for the BBC's *Railway Roundabout* series. Not one was preserved.

Author

Turning 136 tons of locomotive and tender was child's play when the power was supplied from the engine's own steam. On the morning of 5.9.58, 6MT 4–6–2 No. 72003 *Clan Fraser* was being prepared for the 9.00 a.m. train to London (Euston) at Perth shed – class 'A' headlamps were already in position.

Author

Inside the traditional 'straight' shed at Perth on 23.8.61 stood the veteran CR 0–4–4T No. 55124. Built in 1898 with smaller tanks, it managed to survive almost to the end of pre-Grouping steam, having been transferred to 63A from Dumfries in about 1960. It retained the original pattern chimney in preference to the more common stovepipe replacement. The similarity to a LBSCR tank locomotive of the same period is clear.

Author

Also at Perth on 23.8.61 was one of the four-wheel railbuses used on the Gleneagles–Crieff–Comrie branch. There were several different types, but Sc79968 was built by D. Wickham & Co and employed a Meadows diesel unit developing 105 bhp at 1,800 rpm. All the Wickham railbuses were based in Scotland, where their very light weight – only 11¦ tons – gave them unlimited access to any rural route and made few demands on the state of the track. This type seated 44 passengers – notice the 'speed whiskers' and lack of any drawgear.

Author

'Stopped' over the pit inside the diesel shed was No. 54500, one of the final series of Pickersgill 4-4-0 designs for the Caledonian Railway and classified 3P by the LMS (and BR). A Perth engine (63A), No. 54500 in 1961 was one of the last to see active use for it sometimes worked the pick-up goods on the Highland main line to and from Blair Atholl. A sign of things to come was the notice-board below the window (left), setting out the schedule for standard examinations for diesel trains.

Author

Unlike most of the '782' class survivors, 0–6–0T No. 56246 somehow managed to keep its proper Caledonian chimney. Simmering gently in the gasworks' sidings on the outskirts of Perth on 9.9.60, it is likely the elderly engine was waiting for some empty wagons to take back to the main yard, since a brake van stood in the loop alongside. Given the classification 3F, these simple six-coupled tanks were remarkably powerful and surprisingly large.

Author

North of Perth, near the erstwhile junction of Strathord (for Bankfoot), a heavy freight made stirring music on the morning of 9.9.60 bound for Aberdeen. The distinctive sound of a Gresley three-cylinder engine reached the photographer long before the identity of the particular locomotive could be discerned, but it turned out to be one of the small number of class K4 2–6–0s by then shedded at Thornton junction (62A). No. 61994 *The Great Marquess* was benefiting from a slight easing of the gradient after the 1 in 173 before Luncarty; in the 1990s the same engine can be seen restored to LNER apple green livery as No. 3442, based on the Severn Valley Railway.

Author

Near Stanley junction, where Highland and Caledonian tracks joined for the 7 miles to Perth, the 'Up' 'Saint Mungo' (9.30 a.m. from Aberdeen to Glasgow, Buchanan Street) swept round the curve behind class A2 'Pacific' No. 60531 *Bahram* on 9.9.60 amid rural pastures. The Forfar route between Stanley junction and Kinnaber junction – the ex-CR line – had its passenger services withdrawn from 4.9.67.

Author

The 4¾-mile-long branch to Blairgowrie had been part of the Caledonian Railway's empire at the time of Grouping, and did not lose its passenger services until January 1955. Like many Scottish byways the track remained open for occasional freight until the Beeching era swept it all away. On 23.8.61 the Blairgowrie pick-up goods stood in the loop platform at Coupar Angus with a tender-first Stanier 5MT 4–6–0 in charge of just two wagons and a brake van. It is believed the engine was No. 45047, an early domeless example based in the Perth (63A) district. The attractive little station had a number of interesting features, including canopies and supports, both upper- and lower-quadrant signals and a long connecting footbridge. The yard lamp in the centre foreground is worthy of note.

Author

An Edinburgh (St Margarets) engine, class J38 0–6–0 No. 65927 eases a fairly short goods train out of Couper Angus station on 23.8.61 in the direction of Forfar with much hissing and opening of draincocks. Only seven examples of the J38 class were modified with the J39 boiler, this being one of them. The lattice post signals are noteworthy, especially the miniature yard lower-quadrant just to the right of the locomotive.

Author

The Highland Main Line and Aberfeldy Branch

Ballinluig junction was the place where the rivers Tay and Tummel met; it was also the start of the Aberfeldy branch. Pick-up goods trains passed there, having started from Perth and Blair Atholl respectively. On 9.9.60 the southbound goods shuffled away from Ballinluig junction behind one of the splendid Pickersgill 4–4–0s, No. 54486, which still bore signs of being used in the BBC *Railway Roundabout* series with sister engine No. 54485.

Author

Just north of Dunkeld and Birnam wood the B898 road hugs the lineside for several miles towards Balnaguard. On 23.8.61, although most passenger services were diesel-hauled, the 12.17 p.m. from Perth to Inverness was double-headed by D5326 and 'Black 5' 4-6-0 No. 45477 for the northbound assault on Drumochter. This service conveyed through carriages from Glasgow (Buchanan Street) and travelled from Aviemore via Forres, rather than the direct route via Carrbridge – there was even a restaurant car as far as Aviemore.

Author

The 8¾-mile-long branch from Ballinluig junction to Aberfeldy was blessed with a service of five trains each weekday and an extra one on Saturdays; nothing ran on Sundays. The terminus had a small sub-shed for stabling the branch motive power, under Perth (63A). At the junction this intriguing double-armed signal controlled movements on and off the single line, including the imposing bridge on the left of the picture – the one on the right was used by road traffic on the A827.

Author

A surprising amount of goods traffic was handled on the branch. On 23.8.61 the 10.39 a.m. from Ballinluig junction ran as a 'mixed', with ex-CR 0–4–4T No. 55217 giving a spirited performance along the embankment towards Balnaguard. Built in 1910, this was one of the last of the '439' class passenger tanks to remain active, though on a former HR line rather than its native Caledonian.

Author

Half-way along the branch, class 2P 0–4–4T No. 55217 makes a vigorous exit from Grandtully station, trailing one corridor brake carriage plus a dozen assorted goods wagons and guard's van. Of the freight stock, no less than eight are cattle vans, a type of traffic soon to be completely abandoned by BR during the Beeching regime. The train is the 10.39 a.m. from Ballinluig junction to Aberfeldy on 23.8.61.

Author

This study of the arrival of the 10.39 a.m. 'mixed' from Ballinluig at Aberfeldy has a timeless quality about it: Edwardian engine, solid country clientele, cattle lowing in their trucks, inquisitive child. Preservation in all its glory can never be quite as natural as this! The date is 23.8.61, the engine ex-CR 0–4–4T No. 55217. Within a year the old pre-Grouping atmosphere changed and from May 1965 the line was closed for good.

Author

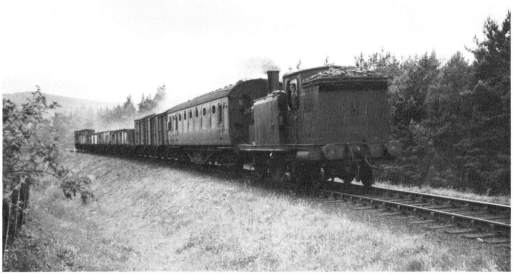

The noon departure from Aberfeldy was allowed thirty-three minutes for the $8\frac{3}{4}$ miles to the junction, instead of the more usual twenty minutes or thereabouts – presumably to enable shunting to take place at the intermediate stations of Grandtully. Despite this generosity, 0–4–4T No. 55217 and its 'mixed' train still managed to overrun on 23.8.61 and the little engine and its load were bustling along the single track in fine style trying to make up time. The location is between Aberfeldy and Grandtully, in the Tay valley.

Author

The northbound pick-up goods from Perth was in the care of a Pickersgill '72' class 4–4–0 on 9.9.60. Having just passed the southbound freight, No. 54500 hooted before heading for the pass of Killiecrankie and on to Blair Atholl, leaving the country junction of Ballinluig to another spell of peaceful inactivity.

Author

Heading into the evening sunlight south of Aviemore, BRCW Type 2 diesel D5324 powered the 5.40 p.m. 'Royal Highlander' from Inverness to London (Euston) on 8.9.60. Behind the Sulzer-engined machine was a HR Royal Mail van, one of the last pre-Grouping vehicles to remain in front-line service, making a bizarre contrast of old and new with the Cairngorm mountains in the right background.

Author

At the same spot a year later, the 'Royal Highlander' boasted not one but *two* of the Sulzer-engined Type 2 diesels – perhaps it was rather ambitious to expect a single 1160 bhp machine to keep time over the switchback Highland main line! On 21.8.61 the engines were D5346 and D5333, while the old Highland Mail coach had been replaced by a new BR Standard design based on the Mark 1 profile.

Author

As the sun settled behind the trees, the crew of Stanier 'Black 5' 4–6–0 No. 44797 prepared their mount for the hard work that lay ahead on the evening of 22.8.61. Before leaving Pitlochry for Inverness, water had to be taken and the coal raked forward in readiness for the gruelling ascent of Drumochter and then Slochd summit after dark, but a Perth engine in good condition was master of the task.

Author

At Aviemore station, a diesel railbus was obliged to share a platform with loco-hauled stock. On 21.8.61 the Speyside service to Boat of Garten and Craigellachie was provided by one of the Park Royal-built vehicles formerly operating in England, M79971. Powered by an AEC six-cylinder engine developing 150 bhp, it seated fifty passengers and weighed 15 tons. This type was immortalized by Airfix who produced a 4 mm scale model kit in plastic for a few shillings!

Author

From Aviemore northwards to Inverness there was a choice of routes: either via Boat of Garten and Forres or the more direct way over Culloden Moor (which included Slochd summit). The 10.00 a.m. from Glasgow (Buchanan Street) used the latter route, and would set down on prior notice at all or any of the wayside stations beyond Aviemore. With motors throttled back, D5127 (built by BR Derby) and D5332 paused briefly at Tomatin on 21.8.61, a quiet little station with typical HR water crane and footbridge. Notice the three bogie vans immediately behind the two diesels, no doubt conveying holiday-makers' luggage.

Author

By 1961 the roundhouse at Inverness (60A) was largely deserted, for the bulk of passenger trains had changed over to diesel haulage. But a handful of steam engines remained, mostly for piloting or local freight duties. Even so, the shed still contained a surprise or two, as for example this 0–6–0PT No. 1646 – one of a pair provided by the Western Region ostensibly to work the Dornoch branch when the native Highland 0–4–4Ts expired.

Author

After a whole morning's work with cotton waste and oily rags by the author and John Courtney Haydon in one of the roundhouse stalls, the sight of class 3P 4-4-0 No. 54495 on the turntable at Inverness was quite rewarding. Built for the Caledonian Railway, by 21.8.61 it was becoming increasingly difficult to find suitable duties for such an engine to do. Nevertheless, with a full tender of coal and plenty of steam in the boiler, the forty-year-old No. 54495 was being turned ready to return to its 'home' shed of Helmsdale (60C) looking spick and span – a classic design in the true Scottish tradition.

Author

If some of the redundant steam engines in Scotland had been sent to Barry in South Wales for scrap, perhaps more of them would have been saved and restored to use once again – but it was not to be. While sister No. 54495 was in steam in the roundhouse nearby, former CR 4–4–0s No. 54493 and 54491 stood outside in all weathers to await the day of judgement. The shed coaling tower stands out against the skyline in the background.

Author

A sad line of redundant engines at Inverness on 20.8.61, few if any of which would turn a wheel again. Among them was McIntosh '782' class 0–6–0T 56305.

Author

Some things don't change . . . While the very latest in diesel multiple units, the Super Sprinter 156 and the Express Sprinter 158, handle an increasing proportion of the services on routes from Inverness (including the Far North line to Wick and Thurso), the station itself remains a cramped terminal with some short curving platforms only capable of handling relatively small trains.

Author

North and West of Inverness

Dingwall marked the junction where the Kyle and Far North lines parted company. In steam days a small sub-shed of Inverness (60A) catered for the twin needs of a yard shunter and station pilot, but with the coming of the diesels the two tasks had to be combined. This meant keeping a pilot engine of sufficient power and resources to be able to substitute for the train engine should a failure occur, hence the retention of a former Caledonian 4–4–0 there, at least in 1960. On 8.9.60 class 3P No. 54487 was the incumbent at Dingwall.

Author

On a cold autumn day with a chill wind blowing up the Cromarty Firth, Pickersgill class 3P 4–4–0 No. 54487 oozed warmth as it waited for some fresh activity in the yard beside the Far North line at Dingwall on 8.9.60. Note the shunter's pole propped against the engine's running plate. With such a loco in steam at a strategic location, such as Dingwall, it was possible to cover most needs for a pilot engine on either the Kyle line or the Far North route should the need arise; meantime, there was always a spot of light shunting to do to keep warm!

Author

This charming study of a brace of 'Caley' 4–4–0s at Dingwall encapsulates much of the appeal of small, remote Highland sheds. At an unknown date in the mid-1950s both Nos 54463 (right) and 54466 were simmering in the sunlight as the shadows lengthened – although built as part of the same batch designed by Pickersgill in 1916, over the intervening years minor differences occurred so that each had its own character.

R.H.G. Simpson

When the two tiny Highland Railway 0–4–4T engines retained for working the branch from The Mound to Dornoch were withdrawn in the mid-fifties, suitable replacements had to be 'borrowed' from the Western Region. Pannier tanks Nos 1646/1649 were almost new then – and must have seemed quite revolutionary in the Far North of Scotland. The Dornoch branch closed in June 1960, but the Panniers did not return home; instead, they were found light shunting to do in place of large-wheeled 4–4–0s. No. 1649 was in steam at Dingwall on 21.8.61, waiting to add some vans to a main line train. The shedplate reads 60C – Helmsdale – which had formerly been responsible for the Dornoch sub-shed.

Author

Made known to a wider public through the TV programme *Great Railway Journeys of the World*, Kyle of Lochalsh has changed little since steam days; the line opened throughout in 1897, though it had reached Strome Ferry by 1870! With the hills of Skye beyond the narrow strip of water to Kyleakin, 37.421 throbs impatiently at the head of the 3.30 p.m. departure to Inverness on 3.9.90. This locomotive has miniature snow ploughs fitted in anticipation of winter conditions, perhaps within a matter of weeks.

Author

Despite rationalization, following the end of steam in Scotland, both main arteries to Kyle of Lochalsh and the Far North remained open. There are even Sunday services, much appreciated by holiday-makers in summer. The Type 2 diesels (classes 26/27) have given way to the Type 3 (class 37) and, by 1990, most trains were provided by Sprinter units. Yet the Kyle line still witnessed some loco-hauled services – for example, 37.156 brought the 12.25 p.m. from Inverness into Kyle of Lochalsh on 3.9.90.

Author

Dugald Drummond's brother Peter designed a class of four small 0–4–4Ts for the Highland Railway in 1905; two survived long enough to enter BR stock in 1948, namely Nos 15051 (55051) and 15053 (55053). The former appears in its pre-Nationalization livery in this broadside view, which illustrates just how small the rear bogie wheels were. The two survivors lingered until 1956/7, continuing to work the Dornoch branch as they had done for many a year, before being replaced by practically brand-new Pannier tanks built at Swindon.

R.H.G. Simpson

Second of the two HR tanks retained for the Dornoch branch, No. 55053 was under repair when photographed inside the Works in the early fifties, sporting a smart lined-black livery – all wheels and axles have been removed. Distinctive features are the dome-mounted safety valves and classic bell-mouthed chimney. The LMS had been somewhat more generous in its power classification than the Southern, because this small engine was rated '1P' whereas the ex-LSWR '02', used to great effect in the Isle of Wight, was only 'OP' – despite almost double the tractive effort of the Adams design!

R.H.G. Simpson

This final study of the Highland Railway in the Far North features that system's last surviving 4-4-0 – No. 54398 *Ben Alder* – probably at Georgemas junction, 147 miles beyond Inverness. Designed by Peter Drummond in 1898, the small 'Ben' class was rebuilt with a Caledonian pattern boiler when the original wore out. In that form but with original chimney, *Ben Alder* was considered for preservation and stored during the fifties and early sixties. Finally, it was deemed unworthy of the National Collection as it was not in 'pure' HR state, and scrapped.

R.H.G. Simpson

Strath Spey and Banffshire

Evidence of the Modernization Plan came early in the Highlands: the delightful Speyside line said farewell to the last Great North of Scotland engines and embraced a four-wheel diesel railbus for its few passengers. On 21.8.61 Park Royal-built M79971 drifted gently into Aviemore forming the 2.45 p.m. from Elgin, framed by an interesting collection of upper-quadrant signals on lattice posts.

Author

After parting from the direct HR route to Inverness, the line again divided upon reaching Boat of Garten station, 5¼ miles out from Aviemore. There, the GNoS system commenced and ran in a north-easterly direction as far as Craigellachie before splitting again; the Forres line turned north after Grantown-on-Spey (West). A visit by the official Inspection Saloon was an important event, to be handled with proper ceremony, so the arrival of McIntosh 3F 0–6–0 No. 57594 at Boat of Garten on 8.9.60 prompted a platform conference.

Author

With the arrival of the afternoon Speyside service at Boat of Garten, the Inspection Saloon could proceed with McIntosh 3F 0–6–0 No. 57594 propelling from the rear. The wicker basket marked 'Tain' stayed on the platform and the signalman had to retrieve the single-line pouch from the railbus by crossing the tracks. The Caledonian engine had come from Inverness via Forres before reversing down the former GNoS route towards Craigellachie. Passengers for Aviemore were able to catch Park Royal railbus Sc79970, looking very smart with correct destination and 'B' headcode (for Branch) displayed – the date was 8.9.60. Both the Speyside and Forres lines were abandoned from mid-October 1965.

Author

The last railbus duty of the day was the 6.45 p.m. from Craigellachie to Aviemore. With another 14½ miles to go, Park Royal railbus No. M79971 paused at Grantown-on-Spey (East) to obtain the next single-line tablet on 22.8.61 while the clouds were gathering over the Cromdale hills. The entire station scene – footbridge, signal cabin and seats – was typical of the former Great North of Scotland Railway.

Author

While provision was made for double track beneath the bridge at Cromdale, it was never needed. In the final years of the Speyside line a four-wheel railbus was sufficient to carry the normal complement of passengers, so Cromdale did not progress beyond a single platform wayside station; it was not even a block-post, despite having a small goods yard and access to the Balmenach Distillery. On 21.8.61 Park Royal railbus No. M79971 purred away from the station when working the final train of the day, the 6.45 p.m. from Craigellachie to Aviemore.

Author

As the passenger service was rather sparce, it was possible for routine maintenance of the Speyside line's track to be carried out on weekdays, rather than invoke such activity on a Sunday. On 22.8.61 a ballast train visited the branch, bringing steam in the shape of a somewhat down-at-heel Standard 2MT 2–6–0, No. 78045, which wheezed through Cromdale disgorging stone chippings from the two hopper wagons where necessary.

Author

The purity of Scottish water encouraged the growth of whisky distilleries in a number of remote places. One of them was about a mile from Cromdale station, along Strath Spey. Balmenach Distillery had its own sidings and connection to the BR system, maintaining a neat little Andrew Barclay 0–4–0ST (No. 2020 of 1936) to handle the rail-borne traffic. On 22.8.61 the green-painted saddle tank trundled an empty coal wagon down from the distillery to the goods yard at Cromdale.

Author

Typical of many small saddle tanks produced by the Kilmarnock works of Andrew Barclay, it served the Speyside company of Scottish Malt Distillers Ltd at its Balmenach Distillery throughout its life. When BR closed the Boat of Garten to Craigellachie section in October 1965 there was no more work – but the 1936-built engine was not scrapped. Now it is based at the private Strathspey Railway, together with similar Barclay 0–4–0ST No. 2073 *Dailuaine* from another of the Speyside distilleries, where both will doubtless find useful employment in preservation not far from their original homes. No. 2020 was pictured when still a 'working' engine at Cromdale on 22.8.61.

Author

Keith shed (61C) in the early 1950s yielded sights like this – former GNoS 4–4–0 No. 62272, which had become LNER class D40. With miniature clerestory on top of the cab, original chimney and a well-filled tender with coal rails it was little changed from Pickersgill's 1899 design. Like the former Caledonian 3P 4–4–0s, the D40 and D41 classes handled both passenger and freight.

R.H.G. Simpson

131

Last of the line, 4–4–0 No. 49 *Gordon Highlander* represents today the only survivor of the Great North of Scotland Railway. Retired by BR as No. 62277 in 1958, it was restored to original condition and made available for special duties (based at Dawsholm shed – 65D) during the early 1960s. In this picture, believed to have been taken at Craigellachie, *Gordon Highlander* has returned to its native haunts on the Speyside line. The locomotive can now be seen displayed in the Glasgow Museum of Transport, together with other Scottish steam engines, tramcars and road vehicles.

R.H.G. Simpson

By 1961 the incumbents of Keith were rather different. Built by North British of Glasgow, a new breed of diesel-electric Type 2 locomotive had appeared, featuring M.A.N. twelve-cylinder engines of either 1,000 or 1,100 bhp. D6156 was one equipped with the more powerful unit, seen in 'as new' condition outside the depot on 22.8.61; just inside can be glimpsed the non-cab end of a Type 1 English Electric diesel (later known as class 20). It is instructive to note that none of the NBL Type 2s exist today (they were to have been class 29). The fold-over headcode discs fitted to these early diesels were an odd feature.

Author

Between Keith and the north coast there used to be a web of railway lines serving the area, but some lost passenger traffic in the thirties while others were abandoned in the fifties. The coastal route from Cairnie junction to Elgin via Buckie lasted until May 1968, having a 6-mile branch from Tillynaught to the county town and port of Banff. Surprisingly, in view of the extent of dieselization elsewhere, the backwater to Banff remained loyal to steam: in pouring rain, the 10.45 a.m. from Tillynaught to Banff was hauled by a Standard 4MT 2–6–0 (No. 76106) on 22.8.61. The two-coach train stopped briefly at Ladysbridge as scheduled, but then the loco had some difficulty 'keeping its feet' when restarting tender-first on the wet rails.

Author

Given only 5 minutes to run-round the train at the terminus, Standard 4MT 2–6–0 No. 76106 was running a bit late with the 11.10 a.m. from Banff to Tillynaught on 22.8.61. With just two coaches in tow, No. 76106 was making a determined effort to regain time as it rattled over the A98 level crossing near Knock Head. Of special interest is the former GNoS lattice-post Home signal on the left: it is a 'sky-arm' version with the warning lamp close to the ground rather than at the top of the post. There was a crossing keeper employed to open and shut the gates by hand at this critical location between Banff and Ladysbridge, and it would seem the traditional wooden gates were never shut across the railway, only across the road, perhaps because of the skew angle. The Banff branch closed in July 1964.

Author

Steam Survivors

Built in 1947 for the LNER, PS *Waverley* is now the last sea-going paddle steamer to be available for cruises 'doon the Watter' and, indeed, elsewhere around Britain's coastline. In this all-action view the banner above the main deck reads: 'Come Cruising to Largs, Millport, Arran'.

Author

Waiting for preservation . . . After its active life with BR had come to an end in about 1960, a novel use was found for former LNER class D49 4-4-0 No. 62712 *Morayshire* – as standby boiler for Slateford Laundry in Edinburgh. It was discovered there, not in use, on 24.8.61 looking shabby but intact. Built at Darlington in 1928, it has been restored to LNER condition as No. 246 and is normally based at Bo'ness on the Firth of Forth.

Author